The Easter Garden

Following in the Footsteps of Jesus

Jenny Hyson

Illustrations by Andy Robb

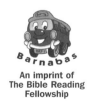

Barnabas

An imprint of
The Bible Reading
Fellowship

Text copyright © Jenny Hyson 1996
Illustrations copyright © Andy Robb 1996

The author asserts the moral right to be
identified as the author of this work.

Published by
The Bible Reading Fellowship
Peter's Way, Sandy Lane West
Oxford OX4 5HG
ISBN 0 7459 3293 2
Albatross Books Pty Ltd
PO Box 320, Sutherland
NSW 2232, Australia
ISBN 0 7324 1558 6

First edition 1996
10 9 8 7 6 5 4 3 2 1 0

All rights reserved

Acknowledgments
Scriptures quoted from the Good News
Bible published by The Bible
Societies/HarperCollins Publishers Ltd UK ©
American Bible Society, 1966, 1971, 1976,
1992.

A catalogue record for this book is
available from the British Library.

Printed and bound in Malta
by Interprint Limited

Introduction

It is fun to walk along a sandy beach or in freshly fallen snow, or even along a muddy pathway and to see what footprints you can make. If you look carefully you might even see where someone, or something has been that way before you!

Footprints can give us clues about who made them by their size and by the direction in which they are going. They can tell us whether they have been made by an animal or a bird or a person. If you follow the footprints they might even take you to whoever made them.

Each day, as you read a page of *The Easter Garden,* and colour in the map, you will discover clues about Jesus. Where he went, who he met, what happened to him and even how very much he loves you.

Through the stories we can discover how to follow in Jesus' footsteps and also how to make footsteps like his for others to follow.

Easter Card Competition

After Easter the Bible Reading Fellowship will be running a competition for the best home-made Easter card. When you have made your card, just send it in to BRF at the address below to arrive by 31 May. Make sure that your name, address and age are written clearly on the back of the card.

There will be 1st, 2nd and 3rd prizes for the best cards in the following age ranges: 5–7, 8–10 and 11–14. Prize winners will be told by post by 31 July. The competition is open to UK residents only.

Enclose an A4 SAE if you would like to have your card returned. Send your card to:

The Bible Reading Fellowship
Peter's Way, Sandy Lane West
Oxford OX4 5HG

Jesus Starts His Journey of Love

Jesus' Baptism
Matthew 3:13, 16–17

At that time Jesus arrived from Galilee and came to John at the Jordan to be baptized by him... As soon as Jesus was baptized, he came up out of the water... Then a voice said from heaven, 'This is my own dear Son, with whom I am pleased.'

Have you ever been to a baptism? You may even remember your own? It's a time of celebration and new beginnings when those being baptized are welcomed into God's family. In some churches people clap in welcome and often the baptism is followed by a party.

Jesus didn't have a party after his baptism, and probably nobody clapped. However, his heavenly Father celebrated and welcomed him. The story tells us that a voice was heard from heaven saying, 'This is my own dear Son, I really love him!'

Jesus' baptism marked a new beginning. At last he was to start the work that God his Father had sent him to do.

Turn to the map in the middle of the book. Can you find the River Jordan? Can you see something else that happened when Jesus came out of the water?

Colour in the first footprint on the map and follow in the footsteps of Jesus as he starts his journey of love—and see what he has to tell you about his loving heavenly Father.

Jesus in the desert

Matthew 4:1-2

Then the Spirit led Jesus into the desert to be tempted by the Devil. After spending 40 days and nights without food, Jesus was hungry. Then the Devil came to him and said, 'If you are God's Son, order these stones to turn into bread.'

Do you sometimes hear that voice inside your head telling you to do something you know is wrong? It may be telling a lie, or taking something without asking, or showing off to impress a friend? We usually know when it's something we shouldn't do because it makes us feel uncomfortable inside. We can choose either to listen to that voice, or to ignore it. But it can be quite a struggle!

Jesus knew that same struggle when he was in the desert. He was there by himself thinking about the best ways of telling the people about God, when the devil came along suggesting that he could show off by performing clever tricks to impress people. Jesus knew that wasn't what God wanted, and chose to ignore the suggestions the devil was making. When the devil knew he couldn't get Jesus to do what he wanted he left him alone. Other people can sometimes try and make us do things we know we shouldn't do, and it can be hard to say, 'No'. Remember how Jesus said 'No' to the devil and how God helped him to know what was the right thing to say.

Find the desert on the map where Jesus said 'No' to the devil. Then colour in footprint 2.

Next time you hear that voice in your head, follow in the footsteps of Jesus and ask God to help you.

Jesus calls his first friends

Mark 1:16–18

As Jesus walked along the shore of Lake Galilee, he saw two fishermen, Simon and his brother Andrew, catching fish with a net. Jesus said to them, 'Come with me, and I will teach you to catch people.' At once they left their nets and went with him.

One of my favourite Winnie the Pooh pictures is of Pooh and Piglet walking along together. Under the picture are the words, 'It's so much friendlier with two.' I like it because it reminds me of how nice it is to have friends to enjoy doing things with as well as to talk to and share things with.

Jesus knew the importance of friends and although he had lots of friends he chose twelve special friends who he asked to travel with him and share what he was doing. Jesus' twelve friends are often called the disciples. They were all very ordinary men, but like the two in our verses today they left what they were doing and followed Jesus wherever he went.

Jesus wanted the disciples to help him tell people about God—he knew he couldn't do it all on his own. Today he still needs our help. He wants us to be his friend and to be friends to one another.

Find Lake Galilee on the map.

Can you see how many fish are in Simon and Andrew's net in the picture? Why not colour in the picture and then follow the footsteps as you colour in footprint 3 on the map?

Jesus goes to a wedding

📖 John 2:1–3, 7–9

There was a wedding in the town of Cana in Galilee. Jesus' mother was there, and Jesus and his disciples had also been invited to the wedding. When the wine had given out, Jesus' mother said to him, 'They have no wine left.'… Jesus said to the servants, 'Fill these jars with water.' They filled them to the brim, and then he told them, 'Now draw some water out and take it to the man in charge of the feast.' They took him the water, which now had turned into wine, and he tasted it.

Weddings are a time of great celebration. In Jesus' time, often the whole village would have been invited to join in. The person organizing the wedding in today's story would have thought that he'd let the family down when the wine ran out. It would look as though they were too mean to provide enough for everyone. What did Jesus do?

Jesus is concerned about everything we do, nothing is unimportant to him. He could have ignored the fact that the wine had run out but he didn't. This first miracle must have been quite a surprise for the disciples. What do you think they thought about their new friend?

🔍 Find the town of Cana on the map and colour it in.

Find six stone jars in the picture and then follow the footsteps as you colour in footprint 4.

7

People come to listen to Jesus

Matthew 4:23–25

Jesus went all over Galilee, teaching in the synagogues, preaching the Good News about the Kingdom, and healing people who had all kinds of disease and sickness. The news about him spread through the whole country of Syria... Large crowds followed him from Galilee and the Ten Towns, from Jerusalem, Judea, and the land on the other side of the Jordan.

Have you ever gone on a journey to see somebody famous? It might have been a member of the Royal Family, or a pop star or your favourite football team. Whatever the occasion it probably caused a lot of excitement and planning! In the time of Jesus, people couldn't just hop in the car, or catch a bus or train to get to places, they would have had to walk.

Yet we read that wherever Jesus went huge crowds would gather. People from all kinds of backgrounds, with all kinds of needs, travelling long distances to see Jesus.

We can't go and listen to Jesus in the same way today, but in the part of the Bible called the Gospels we can read some of the stories that he told.

Look on the map to see how far the people had travelled to come and see Jesus. Then colour in footprint 5.

Imagine that you are listening to your favourite story that Jesus told and draw yourself in the crowd in the picture. Then follow in the footsteps of Jesus by telling your friends stories about him...

Jesus calms a storm

Mark 4:35–39

Jesus said to his disciples, 'Let us go across to the other side of the lake.'… The disciples got into the boat in which Jesus was already sitting, and they took him with them… Suddenly a strong wind blew up, and the waves began to spill over into the boat… Jesus was in the back of the boat, sleeping… The disciples woke him up and said, 'Teacher, don't you care that we are about to die?' Jesus stood up and commanded the wind, 'Be quiet!' and he said to the waves, 'Be still!'

Close your eyes and imagine being in an open boat, tossed about in a storm, with water coming over the sides of the boat and the sails flapping. How do you think you would feel? Lake Galilee often looks calm and still one minute and yet without warning fierce winds can cause a terrible storm. The disciples were very afraid when this happened to them, so afraid that they thought they were going to die. When they saw Jesus asleep in the boat they probably woke him to help them or even maybe to get ready to jump out of the boat! I don't expect they were prepared for what happened next!

When things go wrong it is easy to get in a panic, but Jesus says, 'Trust me.' He promises to be with us even in the middle of the trouble.

Make a model boat like the one caught in the storm. Ask an adult to help you to cut a plastic drinks bottle in half, then using a straw for the mast fasten it into the bottom of the boat with some plasticine. You could use a scrap of material to make a sail and two people made out of pipe cleaners for you and Jesus.

On the map, draw a picture of the boat on Lake Galilee.

Next time you are afraid think about your boat and remember that Jesus is there with you. Have you coloured in footprint number 6?

9

Along the Road

Jesus meets a little boy with a picnic

John 6:5, 8–11

Jesus looked round and saw that a large crowd was coming to him, so he asked Philip, 'Where can we buy enough food to feed all these people?'... Andrew... said, 'There is a boy here who has five loaves of barley bread and two fish. But they will certainly not be enough for all these people.'
'Make the people sit down,' Jesus told them... Jesus took the bread, gave thanks to God, and distributed it to all the people... He did the same with the fish, and they all had as much as they wanted.

We aren't told whether the little boy in our story today complained about sharing his picnic, but we do know that in sharing not only did he have enough to eat but so did everyone else!

I met a little boy who'd collected pennies in a Smartie tube for the children who live on the streets in Guatemala. When his pennies were added to pennies collected by other children there was over £7,000. The little boy said, 'I never knew my few pennies could help to make so much.' Some problems can seem so big that we think we can't do anything about them, but these stories show us that if we offer to help in little ways we can make a big difference.

Find the crowd of people with the boy who gave his picnic to Jesus on the map and colour them in. Don't forget to colour footprint number 7.

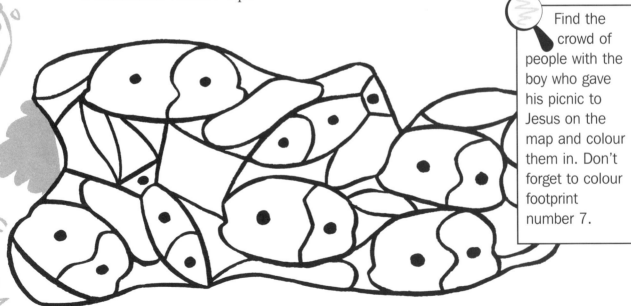

Colour in the spots on the picture above to find the five loaves and two fish. Follow in the footsteps of Jesus and help someone today—you could make a big difference to their day.

Jesus meets four friends

📖 Mark 2:1–4

Jesus went back to Capernaum… So many people came together that there was no room left… Four men arrived, carrying a paralysed man to Jesus. Because of the crowd, however, they could not get the man to him. So they made a hole in the roof right above the place where Jesus was. When they had made an opening, they let the man down, lying on his mat.

The flat-roofed houses in Capernaum would have had stairs leading up the outside onto the roof, and it was up these that the four friends carried the paralysed man. Everyone in the house must have been very surprised suddenly to see the sky and a man being lowered through the roof on a mattress. Jesus recognized how much the friends cared for the man and how they trusted Jesus to make him better. If you read the rest of the story you'll see that Jesus told the man to 'Get up, pick up your mat, and go home!' Can you imagine the laughter and excitement of the friends as they walked home together!

Think about your friends: do you always want what is best for them? If your friend was sick or sad what would you do? You couldn't take them to Jesus in the same way that the friends took the paralysed man, but you could take your friend to Jesus in a different way, by praying for them.

Can you find the house in Capernaum on the map? Draw in the hole the four friends made in the roof.

Colour in the four friends—and the man who was healed—going home together on the picture and then follow the footsteps by colouring footprint 8.

The Good Samaritan

Luke 10:30, 33–34

Jesus said, 'There was once a man who was going down from Jerusalem to Jericho when robbers attacked him, stripped him, and beat him up, leaving him half dead... A Samaritan who was travelling that way came upon the man, and when he saw him, his heart was filled with pity. He went over to him, poured oil and wine on his wounds and bandaged them; then he... took him to an inn, where he took care of him.

Have you ever shouted for help and people have ignored you and carried on with what they are doing? How does it make you feel? Sometimes help can come from people we least expect, as in today's story.

The road from Jerusalem to Jericho winds its way among the hills and is a very deserted place—cries for help could go unheard. In the story that Jesus told, two people passed by and ignored the man's cries for help. Maybe they were too busy or didn't want to get involved or even just didn't care. Only the man from Samaria stopped to help.

What excuses do you sometimes give for not helping someone? Are you sometimes too busy or is it because the person is not your friend? Jesus wants us to help not just our friends and the people we like, but also those who we find it difficult to get along with.

On the map find the route from Jerusalem to Jericho.

Then follow in the footsteps of Jesus—he didn't just help those people he liked, he helped everyone. Don't forget to colour in today's footprint.

Jesus meets ten lepers

Luke 17:11–17

As Jesus made his way to Jerusalem, he went along the border between Samaria and Galilee. He was going into a village when he was met by ten men suffering from a dreaded skin disease. They… shouted, 'Jesus! Master! Take pity on us!'

Jesus saw them and said to them, 'Go and let the priests examine you.' On the way they were made clean. When one of them saw that he was healed, he came back, praising God in a loud voice… Jesus said, 'There were ten men who were healed; where are the other nine?'

Have you ever had measles or chickenpox and had to stay away from your friends in case you pass on your spots to them? It can feel very miserable and lonely, can't it? The men in our story had a terrible skin disease called leprosy. Unlike measles it didn't get better, and they were forced to live right away from their family and friends outside the village. Imagine having to live away from those who you love and being called 'unclean'. No wonder when the men saw Jesus they asked him to have pity on them.

Jesus didn't turn his back on the men or make fun of them. Instead he made them well again. When people saw others as different and not worth bothering with, Jesus showed that he cared for them, he treated everyone the same.

On the map find the man who went back to say thank you to Jesus.

Can you find the other nine men hidden in the picture? When you've found them, follow in the footsteps of Jesus by caring for those who are being ignored and left out today. Have you coloured in today's footprint?

Jesus meets some children

Mark 10:13-14, 16

Some people brought children to Jesus for him to place his hands on them, but the disciples scolded the people. When Jesus noticed this, he was angry and said to his disciples, 'Let the children come to me, and do not stop them, because the Kingdom of God belongs to such as these... Then he took the children in his arms, placed his hands on each of them, and blessed them.

Imagine going to see somebody you really wanted to see, having to wait a long time to get to the front of the line and then being sent away because you were too small. How do you think you would feel? Now imagine that having been sent away the person you were wanting to see called out, 'Wait a minute! Come here! I really want to see you.' I expect you would feel really happy.

It wasn't really surprising that the disciples tried to send the children away from Jesus, as in those days children were not thought to be very important. But with Jesus, however small you are you need never feel unimportant, for he thinks you are very special.

Find Jesus with the children on the map and colour them in.

Imagine you were one of the children who Jesus called to him, what would you like to tell him?
He still listens today, so why not draw yourself in the picture and talk to him? Then colour in today's footprints.

14

Jesus visits Martha and Mary

Luke 10:38–40

As Jesus and his disciples went on their way, he came to a village where a woman named Martha welcomed him in her home. She had a sister called Mary, who sat down at the feet of the Lord and listened to his teaching. Martha was upset over all the work she had to do, so she came and said, 'Lord don't you care that my sister has left me to do all the work by myself? Tell her to come and help me!'

I wonder how many times in a day you say 'It's not fair'? That's what Martha said to Jesus when he came to visit. 'It's not fair,' she said, 'that Mary is sitting talking to you while I'm doing all the work.' But instead of telling Mary to go and help her sister, Jesus told Martha to stop feeling worried and cross. Sometimes we can be so busy rushing round that we don't have time to stop and think about God. When your best friend comes to visit I expect you enjoy doing things together or sitting talking together. God wants to be our friend and he wants us to have time to talk to him too. That's why Jesus didn't tell Mary off; he knew it was really important to spend time together.

Look on the map and see if you can find Martha and Mary's house in Bethany. It's near today's footprint.

Draw a picture of Martha cooking the dinner in the picture and then follow in the footsteps of Jesus by finding time to talk to him.

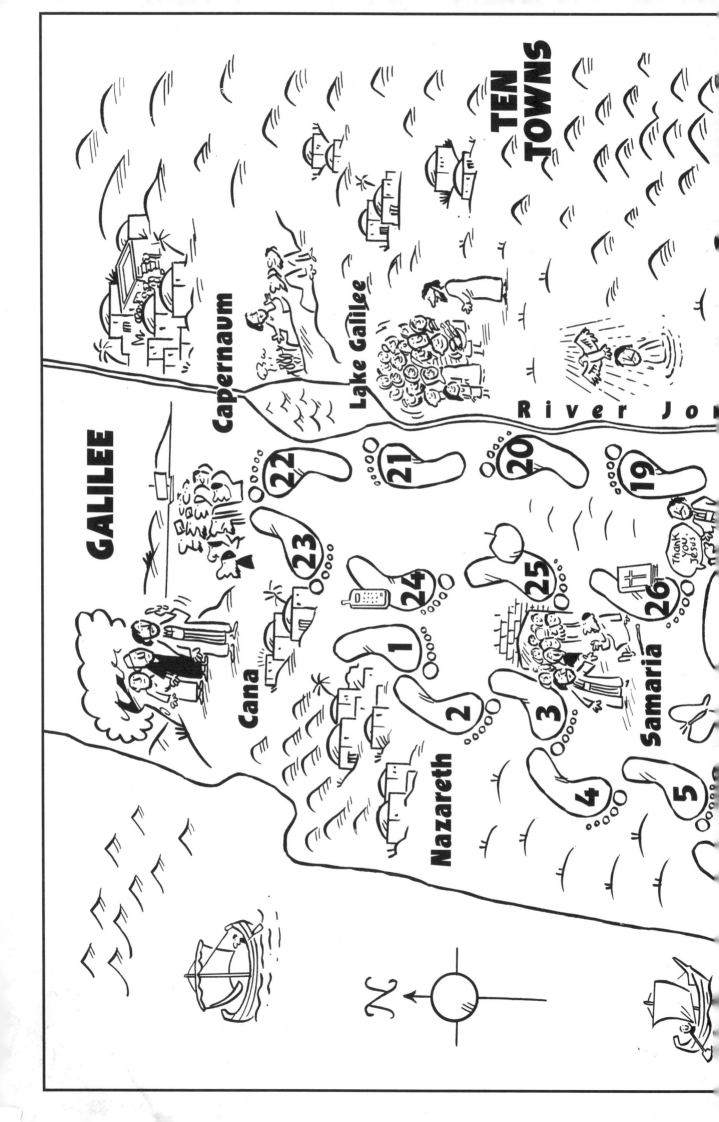

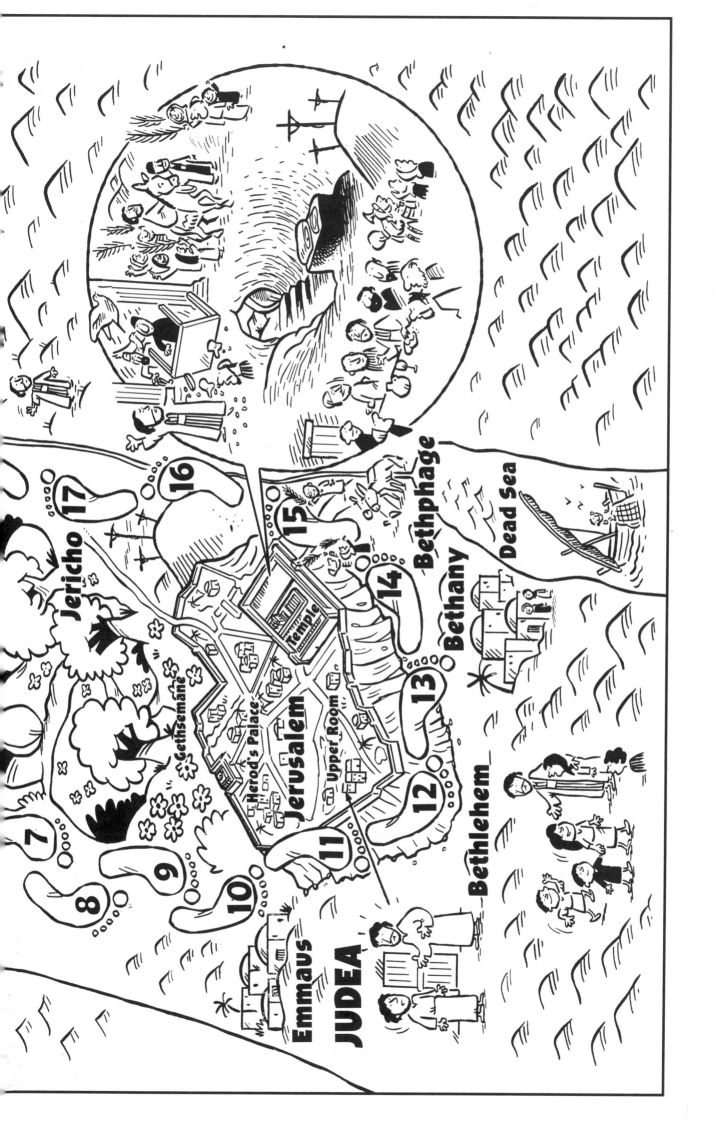

Jesus sends for a donkey

Matthew 21:1–2

As Jesus and his disciples approached Jerusalem, they came to Bethphage at the Mount of Olives. Then Jesus sent two of the disciples on ahead with these instructions: 'Go to the village there ahead of you, and at once you will find a donkey tied up with her colt beside her. Untie them and bring them to me.'

Have you ever been on a treasure hunt where you are given a list of instructions to follow? If you follow the instructions very carefully they will lead you to the right spot and you will find what you are looking for. The two disciples must have thought they were on a 'donkey hunt' when they set off with their instructions!

The disciples had been with Jesus for about three years, and in that time had seen him do and say some amazing things. They had seen him change the water into wine at the wedding in Cana, and heal many sick people. I expect when he sent the two disciples off with the instructions to bring back a donkey they wondered what he was going to do next! However they had grown to trust Jesus and so went and found everything as he had said.

Can you find Bethphage on the map? Colour in the donkey and her colt.

Help the two disciples to find the way to the donkey and her colt through the maze and then colour in today's footprint.

Jesus the King

 Matthew 21:6–9

So the disciples went and did what Jesus had told them to do: they brought the donkey and the colt, threw their cloaks over them, and Jesus got on. A large crowd of people spread their cloaks on the road while others cut branches from the trees and spread them on the road. The crowds… began to shout, '… God bless him who comes in the name of the Lord!'

Wherever Jesus went he always attracted a large crowd and this day on the journey into Jerusalem was no exception. Crowds gathered cheering and waving branches from the trees calling for Jesus to be their king. Whilst Jesus made many friends, he also made many enemies amongst the religious leaders of the day and they were already plotting to have Jesus killed.

This week we're following Jesus in the last week of his life—it's sometimes called Holy Week. As you follow in Jesus' footsteps you'll see the way Jesus continued to love people even though many of them let him down.

The branches people spread on the road in front of Jesus were probably from the palm trees. In some churches on Palm Sunday people are given crosses made of palm to remind them of today's story.

> You need 2 strips of card, 1cm x 27cm and 1cm x 35cm.

1. Mark 1cm, 2cm, 3cm, 9cm and 21 cm on the short strip.

2. Fold at each mark.

3. Flatten short strip and tuck one end of long strip into middle of folds.

4. Loop other end of long strip through gap behind first end and pull tight.

5. Make a fold 6cm along long strip.

6. Push long end back through gap up to the fold.

Look on the map and find the road along which Jesus rode into Jerusalem. Then colour in today's footprint.

You could make palm crosses out of coloured paper and give them to your friends to show that you are following in Jesus footsteps. . .

Jesus is angry

Matthew 21:12–13

Jesus went into the Temple and drove out all those who were buying and selling there. He overturned the tables of the moneychangers and stools of those who sold pigeons, and said to them, 'It is written in the Scriptures that God said, "My Temple will be called a house of prayer." But you are making it a hideout for thieves!'

Imagine going to church on a Sunday and not being allowed in unless you had special money to put in the collection plate and a lamb or a pigeon to give to the priest, to say you were sorry to God.

This is what happened when people went to the temple in Jerusalem and this is why Jesus was so angry. The temple courtyard was looking more like a market place and the people visiting the temple were being cheated by those who were selling. No wonder Jesus was so angry. He was hurt and upset that people were behaving badly, in God's special place.

On the map follow Jesus into the temple courtyard. What did Jesus say the moneychangers had turned God's house into?

Look at the picture and see if you can find five lost pennies, three pigeons that have flown away, and two broken stools. Then colour the footprint for today.

Jesus washes the disciples' feet

John 13:2, 6–9

Jesus and his disciples were at supper… Jesus rose from the table, took off his outer garment, and tied a towel round his waist… He came to Simon Peter, who said to him… 'Never at any time will you wash my feet!' 'If I do not wash your feet,' Jesus answered, 'You will no longer be my disciple.' Simon Peter answered, 'Lord, do not wash only my feet, then! Wash my hands and head, too!'

I wonder if when you are at school and it is time for dinner your teacher tells you to go and wash your hands? A similar thing is happening in our story today, though it may seem a bit strange that Jesus is going to wash the disciples' feet!

Where Jesus lived the roads were very dusty and so when you went for a meal with someone it was likely that a servant would come and wash the dust of the road from your feet. It was because it was usually the job of the servant to do this that Simon Peter got so upset when Jesus went to wash his feet.

Jesus wanted his disciples to learn an important lesson: that following him means being like a servant to others. Always thinking of others' needs before our own, being thoughtful and sharing what we have can be ways we 'serve' one another. In what other ways can you follow in Jesus' footsteps and serve your friends?

On the map see if you can find the house with the upper room where Jesus washed the disciples' feet. Colour in footprint 16.

Dear Lord Jesus...

Follow in Jesus' footsteps and write a prayer in the footprint asking Jesus to help you to think of ways of being kind to others.

Jesus shares a special supper with his friends

Matthew 26:20; Luke 22:17-19

When it was evening, Jesus and the twelve disciples sat down to eat... Then Jesus took a cup, gave thanks to God, and said, 'Take this and share it among yourselves...' Then he took a piece of bread, gave thanks to God, broke it, and gave it to them, saying, 'This is my body, which is given for you. Do this in memory of me.'

When somebody we love dies, it is good to talk about them and to remember special times that were shared together. The disciples did not know when they were preparing the Passover supper that it would be the last meal they would have with Jesus. But Jesus knew, and he wanted to do something that they would always remember.

Today's story might remind you of something we do in church. Ever since Jesus died people have remembered how, just before he was killed, Jesus shared the bread and wine with his disciples and told them to do the same as a way of remembering him.

Did you find the upper room on the map? Can you picture the place where you have shared a special meal with your friends and family?

Draw in the twelve disciples as they share the special meal with Jesus. You could draw yourself at the table as well, and then colour in today's footprint.

Jesus cries

Mark 14:32–37

They came to a place called Gethsemane, and Jesus said to his disciples, 'Sit here while I pray.' He took Peter, James, and John with him… and he said to them, '… Stay here and keep watch.' He went a little farther on, threw himself on the ground, and prayed that, if possible, he might not have to go through that time of suffering. 'Father… Yet not what I want, but what you want' Then he returned and found the three disciples asleep. He said to Peter, 'Simon, are you asleep? Weren't you able to stay awake even for one hour?'

After the special supper together, Jesus took the disciples to a quiet garden to pray. He was feeling particularly sad and afraid as he knew he was soon to die. During supper Jesus had told the disciples that very shortly they would let him down and run away, but they had all denied it. Have you ever been let down by someone you trusted? It is not a very nice feeling is it? Do you think Jesus felt let down by the disciples when they went to sleep instead of keeping watch?

If you read on in the story you will see what happens next. Into the quiet garden came soldiers ready to arrest Jesus. Leading the soldiers was Judas one of the disciples—was he going to let Jesus down as well?

Can you find the Garden of Gethsemane on the map?

Can you see the three disciples who fell asleep in the picture? Think back over this last week. Is there someone you have let down? Why not follow in the footsteps of Jesus by saying you are sorry? Then you can colour in today's footprint.

The day Jesus died

Luke 23:33–34, 38, 44–46

When they came to the place called 'The Skull', they crucified Jesus... Jesus said, 'Forgive them, Father! They don't know what they are doing.'
Above him were written these words: 'This is the King of the Jews' It was about twelve o'clock when the sun stopped shining and darkness covered the whole country until three o'clock... Jesus cried out in a loud voice, 'Father! In your hands I place my spirit!' He said this and died.

When Jesus died, his friends were very, very sad. It seemed like the end of everything. Jesus had loved and helped so many people and now he was dead. It must have been a terrible day.

Often at Easter time people buy 'hot cross buns'. On the top of the bun is the pattern of a cross. The cross is a reminder of how Jesus died—not just for people who lived 2,000 years ago, but for everyone, including you and me!

Why did Jesus die? Because he loved us so very much—he wanted to make sure his footsteps led us to God.

Jesus was crucified outside the city walls of Jerusalem. On the map follow the path that he might have taken from Herod's palace to the place where he was crucified.

Trace the cross shape on to a piece of card. Cut it out and decorate it. Down the centre you could write the words, 'Jesus died for me.' Then colour in today's footprint.

24

A day of waiting

📖 Matthew 27:57–61

When it was evening, a rich man from Arimathea arrived; his name was Joseph, and he was a disciple of Jesus. He went to Pilate and asked for the body of Jesus... So Joseph took it, wrapped it in a new linen sheet, and placed it in his own tomb, which he had just recently dug out of solid rock. Then he rolled a large stone across the entrance to the tomb and went away. Mary Magdalene and the other Mary were sitting there, facing the tomb.

Jesus died on the evening of the Jewish sabbath, a time when Jews were not allowed to work or travel. So it was that the two Marys followed Joseph to watch where he buried Jesus, knowing that after the sabbath they would go to the tomb to anoint Jesus' body with special ointments.

All of that first day Jesus' friends had to wait. They hid behind closed doors, maybe afraid in case the soldiers who had arrested Jesus would come after them as well. I wonder what they were feeling? What did they talk about? Unlike us, they didn't know that this was not the end of the story...

Have you noticed how, when spring comes, the leaves begin to grow on the trees, flowers come out, and even the birds seem to have a different song? At Easter time you could collect some stones and twigs, moss and soil and then, using a tray or small box, make your own Easter garden. Use the stones to make the tomb, and don't forget to roll a round stone over the entrance. You could make some pipe-cleaner figures for the two Marys.

Find the Easter garden on the map and draw some flowers, and birds singing in the garden.

👣 **Next time you are out walking listen to see if you can hear the birds singing. Have you coloured in today's footprint?**

Beyond the Garden

Easter Day

📖 Mark 16:1–4

After the Sabbath was over, Mary Magdalene, Mary the mother of James, and Salome brought spices to go and anoint the body of Jesus. Very early on Sunday morning, at sunrise, they went to the tomb. On the way they said to one another, 'Who will roll away the stone for us from the entrance to the tomb?'… Then they looked up and saw that the stone had already been rolled back.

Weeks before Easter the shops begin to fill up with chocolate Easter eggs, yellow chicks and fluffy bunnies, and we might easily forget that Easter is really about today's story of that very first Easter Sunday.

When the three women went to the tomb early in the morning they must have still been feeling very sad. They were also worried as to how they were going to move the huge stone that had been rolled over the entrance to the tomb so that they could anoint the body of Jesus. Imagine then their surprise to find the stone rolled away! They must have been afraid when they saw that the body of Jesus had disappeared. But their fear turned to joy at the news that Jesus had been raised from the dead. I expect they ran all the way back to tell the disciples what they had seen and what they had been told!

Can you find the garden tomb on the map?

Why not make an Easter card that shows which part of the Easter story is special to you? You can send your card in to our competition: the details are on page 3. Don't forget to colour today's footprint.

An upstairs room

John 20:19, 24–27

It was late that Sunday evening, and the disciples were gathered together behind locked doors… then Jesus came and stood among them…

One of the twelve disciples, Thomas… was not with them when Jesus came. So the other disciples told him, 'We have seen the Lord!' Thomas said to them, 'Unless I see the scars of the nails in his hands and put my finger on those scars and my hand in his side, I will not believe.'

A week later the disciples were together again indoors, and Thomas was with them. The doors were locked, but Jesus came and stood among them and said, 'Peace be with you.' Then he said to Thomas, 'Put your finger here, and look at my hands.'

Have you ever said 'I'll believe it when I see it' about something your friends have told you? It can be hard to believe something unless you see it for yourself, can't it? Notice what happens when Jesus appears to Thomas.

He does not laugh at him or even get angry with him—he just invites Thomas to see for himself. Sometimes it can be hard for us to believe all that we hear about Jesus. Further on in today's story Jesus says to Thomas, 'Do you believe because you see me? How happy are those who believe in me without seeing me!'

Why not ask Jesus to help you to trust in him even though you can't see him? Then colour in today's footprint.

Find the picture of Jesus and Thomas on the map and colour it in.

Breakfast on the beach

John 21:1, 3–4, 6–7, 10, 12

After this, Jesus appeared once more to his disciples at Lake Tiberias. This is how it happened…
Simon Peter said to the others, 'I am going fishing.' 'We will come with you,' they told him. So they went out in a boat, but all that night they did not catch a thing. As the sun was rising, Jesus stood on the water's edge, but the disciples did not know that it was Jesus… He said to them, 'Throw your net out on the right side of the boat, and you will catch some.' So they threw the net and could not pull it back in, because they had caught so many fish. The disciple whom Jesus loved said to Peter, 'It is the Lord!' When Peter heard that it was the Lord, he… jumped into the water… Then Jesus said… 'Bring some of the fish you have just caught.'… 'Come and eat.'

I wonder if you have ever had a breakfast picnic on the beach, very early in the morning? For the disciples in today's story it must have been a special picnic, but for Peter it was probably a breakfast he would never forget!

After Jesus had been arrested, Peter said three times that he didn't know Jesus. He'd let Jesus down and then it was too late to say he was sorry.

Now here is Jesus at this special picnic breakfast, asking Peter three times if he loved him. Jesus wanted Peter to know that he had forgiven him for letting him down, and he also wanted Peter to know that he was trusting him to go on telling others about Jesus.

On the map find Jesus and his disciples having breakfast on the beach and colour in today's footprint.

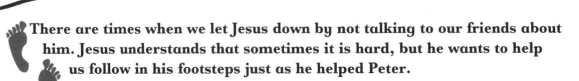

There are times when we let Jesus down by not talking to our friends about him. Jesus understands that sometimes it is hard, but he wants to help us follow in his footsteps just as he helped Peter.

Talking to Jesus

Luke 11:2–4

Jesus said... 'When you pray, say this: "Father: May your name be honoured; may your Kingdom come. Give us day by day the food we need. Forgive us our sins, for we forgive everyone who does us wrong. And do not bring us to hard testing." '

Some of my friends live a long way away and I cannot get to see them very often. The telephone is a good way of saying hello and finding out what they have been doing.

Even though we cannot see Jesus, he wants us to talk to him—to say hello and to tell him what we have been doing. He wants to know when we are worried or sad, just as we might tell a friend. Remember that when you use the telephone it is usually a two-way conversation and you have to listen to the other person. Jesus wants us to learn to listen to him—so don't 'put the phone down on him' when you have finished talking! Learn to listen.

On the map find the footprint with a telephone in it and colour it in.

Join up the dots to find the telephone in the picture above.

29

Growing more like Jesus

Luke 6:43–45

'A healthy tree does not bear bad fruit, nor does a poor tree bear good fruit. Every tree is known by the fruit it bears... A good person brings good out of the treasure of good things in his heart.'...

I've got an apple tree in my garden and one year it seemed to be growing beautiful juicy cooking apples. They certainly looked good on the outside! However when I came to cut them in half, I found that the inside of the apple was all black.

Jesus said we can be a bit like my apple tree. He says that the kind of person we are is not shown by what we look like on the outside but how we behave towards others. He calls it the treasure of our heart.

People followed Jesus not because he was rich, famous or clever but because he was kind, forgiving and treated everyone the same. Jesus wants us to follow in his footsteps by being kind to other people.

On the map find the footprint with the fruit on it and colour it in.

joy fighting patient caring

love impatient selfish

kind peace hate

spiteful

unkind angry generous

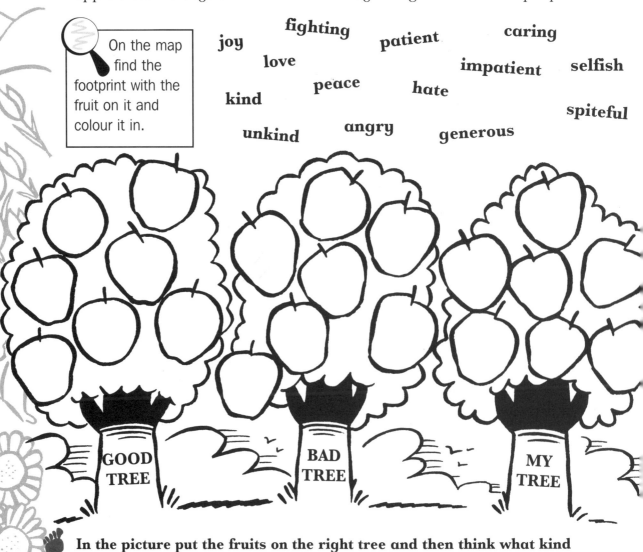

GOOD TREE

BAD TREE

MY TREE

In the picture put the fruits on the right tree and then think what kind of fruit you are growing on the tree of your heart.

Finding out more

 John 21:25

Now, there are many other things that Jesus did. If they were all written down one by one, I suppose that the whole world could not hold the books that would be written.

The Bible tells us of the many things that Jesus did and taught. Yet John says there is still more to tell. So much more that the world could not hold all the books that would be written. What a lot of books!

If we want to find out more about Jesus, the Bible is a good place to begin. Jesus told many stories about his heavenly Father and about heaven. He also told us how special we are to God.

As we read the stories in the Bible and put the pieces of the stories together, we can begin to build up a picture for ourselves of what Jesus is like, and how he wants us to follow him. It is a bit like putting the pieces of a jigsaw puzzle together—the more pieces we fit together the more of the picture we will be able to see.

On the map find the footprint with a Bible in it and colour it in. Where else could we find out more about Jesus?

Look at the jigsaw pieces. If they were put together which of Jesus' stories would they tell? What did you learn about Jesus from that story?

31

Following in the footsteps of Jesus

📖 John 10:2–5

The man who goes in through the gate is the shepherd of the sheep... The sheep hear his voice as he calls his own sheep by name, and he leads them out. When he has brought them out, he goes ahead of them, and the sheep follow him, because they know his voice.

Jesus told many stories about shepherds and their sheep— probably because they were a familiar sight around the hills of Israel, and because they give a good picture of how Jesus wants to take care of us.

Where Jesus lived, the shepherd would have stayed with his sheep all day and night to protect them from wild animals, leading them to safe places to feed and drink. Our final Bible verse tells us how the sheep trust the shepherd, recognizing his voice and following him wherever he leads them.

As we have followed in the footsteps of Jesus through the pages of this book, we have seen how much Jesus cares for ordinary people like you and me.

> You could finish colouring in the map today. The last footprint on the map has a space for you to write your name in.

Jesus called himself the good shepherd because he wants us to learn to trust him and to follow in his footsteps every day.

32